A FRIENDLY
UNIVERSE

SAYINGS TO INSPIRE AND CHALLENGE YOU

JEREMY P. TARCHER • PENGUIN

A MEMBER OF PENGUIN GROUP (USA)

NEW YORK

A FRIENDLY UNIVERSE

BYRON KATIE

JEREMY P. TARCHER • PENGUIN
Published by the Penguin Group
Penguin Group (USA) LLC
375 Hudson Street
New York, New York 10014

USA • Canada • UK • Ireland • Australia
New Zealand • India • South Africa • China

penguin.com
A Penguin Random House Company

Most Tarcher/Penguin books are available at special quantity discounts for bulk purchase for sales promotions, premiums, fund-raising, and educational needs. Special books or book excerpts also can be created to fit specific needs. For details, write: Special.Markets@us.penguingroup.com

Library of Congress Cataloging-in-Publication Data

Katie, Byron.
A friendly universe : sayings to inspire and challenge you / Byron Katie.
p.   cm.
ISBN 978-0-399-16693-8
1. Conduct of life—Quotations, maxims, etc.   I. Title.
BJI589.K38   2013   2013035203
158.1—dc23

Printed in China
3 5 7 9 10 8 6 4 2

Book design by Hans Wilhelm and Judy Henderson

To Max and Ben Lewis,
with love.
B.K.

The Work of Byron Katie

Identify a stressful situation; then identify a thought you were believing about the person in the situation. (For example: "He doesn't appreciate what I do for him.")

Then question that thought, using the following questions.

The Four Questions:

1. Is it true?

2. Can you absolutely know that it's true?

3. How do you react, what happens, when you believe that thought?

4. Who or what would you be without the thought?

Then turn the thought around and find examples for each turnaround.

*(The full Worksheet is available free of charge at **thework.com**.)*

When you realize that the nature of everything is good and that good is everything, you don't need this Work. There is a (bogus) story that Einstein said there is only one important question to answer: "Is the universe friendly?" In 1986 I woke up to an answer of Yes, and I wasn't even aware that there was a question. I just immediately, in a single moment, understood. I saw that the entire universe is kind. The four questions and turnarounds are the internal path to this understanding. Whenever you don't understand, do The Work and welcome yourself to your own kind nature.

Byron Katie

There's no mistake in the universe. Everything is *for* you—the universe is friendly. And any thought that opposes that is going to feel like stress. So if you oppose it, you lose—but only 100 percent of the time. Reality rules. It will not move for you. And I love that, because you can trust it. Right here, right now, is where you have the power. When you're not arguing with reality, you're clear, and everything you're to do is possible right here, and the options are unlimited.

Reality is always kinder than the story we tell about it.

We are really alive only when we live in nonbelief—open, waiting, trusting, and loving to do what appears in front of us now.

The miracle of love comes to us in the
presence of the uninterpreted moment.

Love says, "I love you no matter what."
Love says, "You're fine the way you are."
And that is the only thing that can heal;
that is the only way you can join. If you
think he's supposed to be different from
what he is, you don't love him. In that
moment you love who he's going to be
when you're through manipulating him.
He is a throwaway until he matches
your image of him.

Personalities don't love;
they want something.

If I had a prayer,
it would be this:
"God, spare me from
the desire for love,
approval, or appreciation.
Amen."

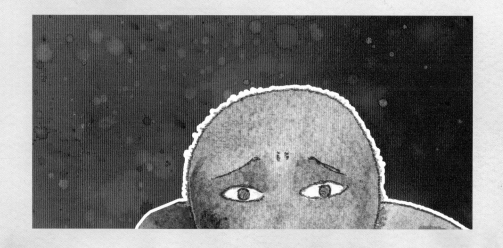

No one can hurt me—

that's my *job.*

The worst thing that has ever happened is an uninvestigated thought.

Sanity doesn't suffer, ever.

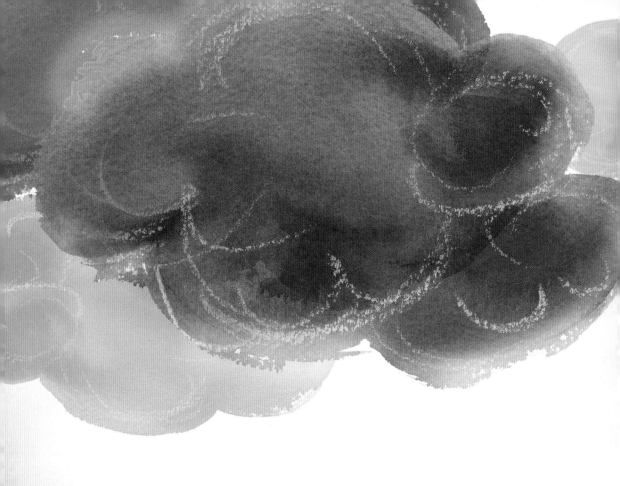

All the suffering that anybody has ever experienced is in the past.
This moment now is a state of grace.

You either believe your stressful thoughts

or you question them—there's no other choice.

Everything happens *for* me, not *to* me.

An unquestioned mind
is
the world
of suffering.

A lover of what is looks forward to everything: life, death, disease, loss, earthquakes, bombs, anything the mind might be tempted to call "bad." Life will bring us everything we need, to show us what we haven't undone yet. Nothing outside ourselves can make us suffer. Except for our unquestioned thoughts, every place is paradise.

The teacher you need
is the person you're living with.

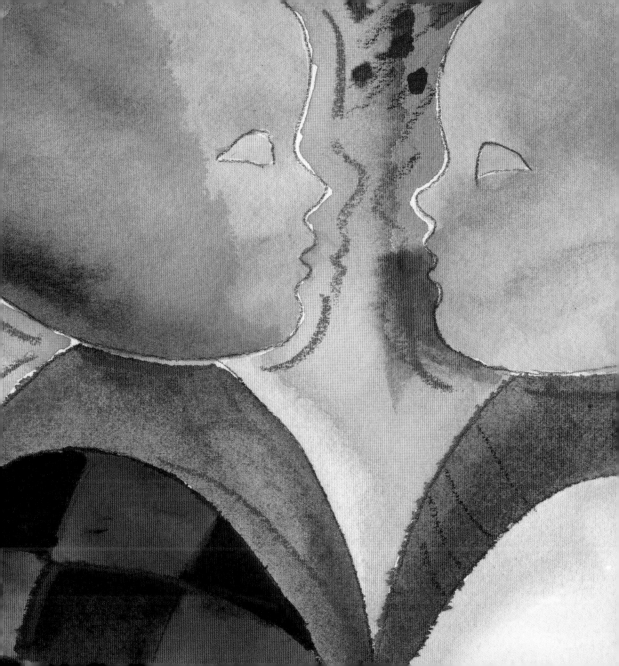

I don't let go of
stressful thoughts—
I question them.
Then *they* let go of *me.*

Confusion is the only suffering.

*You move
totally away
from reality
when you
believe that
there is a
legitimate
reason
to suffer.*

If I lose all my money, good.
If I get cancer, good.
If my husband leaves me, good.
If he stays, that's good too.
Who wouldn't always say yes to reality
if that's what you're in love with?
What can happen that I wouldn't
welcome with all my heart?

Reality is God,
because it rules.

I hear people say that compassion means feeling someone else's pain, as if that were even possible. And how are you most present, most available—when you're in pain or when you're clear and happy? When someone is hurting, why would they want you to be hurting too? Wouldn't they rather have you totally present and available?

You can't feel another person's pain.
You can feel only your projection of it.

Forgiveness means realizing that what happened, didn't.

"I don't know" is my favorite position.

*Stress is an alarm clock
that lets you know you've
attached to something
that's not true for you.*

Give yourself permission to be a fool.

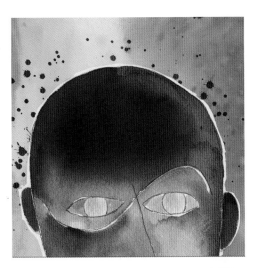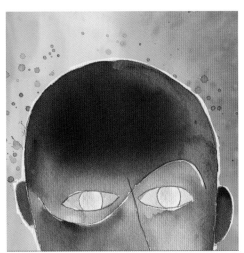
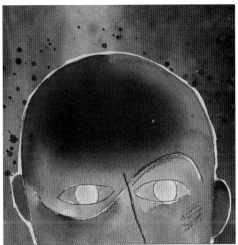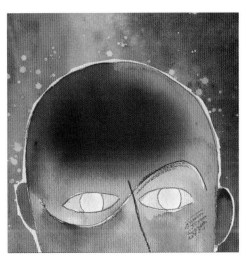

*I'm a lover of what is,
not because I'm a spiritual person
but because it hurts when
I argue with reality.*

Thoughts aren't personal.
They just appear, like raindrops.
Would you argue with a raindrop?

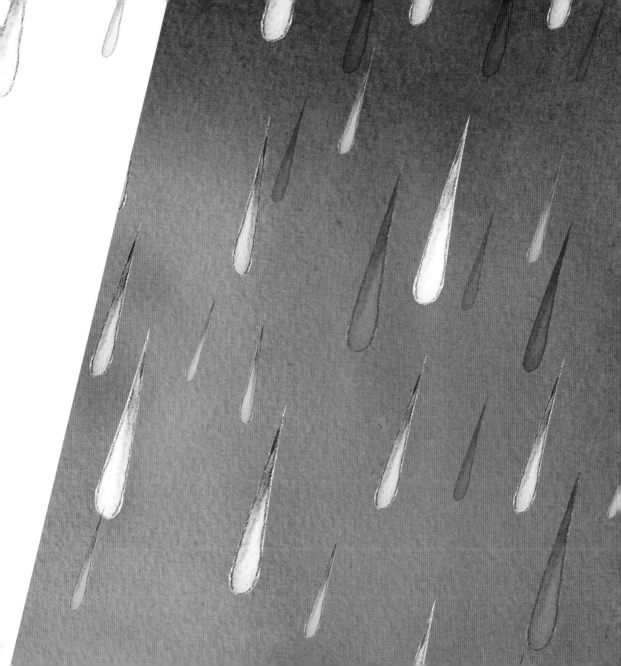

Reality unfolds perfectly. Whatever happens is good. I see people and things, and when it comes to me to move toward them or away from them, I move without argument, because I have no believable story about why I shouldn't; it's always perfect. A decision would give me less, always less. So "it" makes its own decision, and I follow. And what I love is that it's always kind. If I had to name the experience in a word, I would call it "gratitude." Living, breathing gratitude. I am a receiver, and there's nothing I can do to stop grace from coming in.

We never make a decision. When the time is right, the decision makes itself.

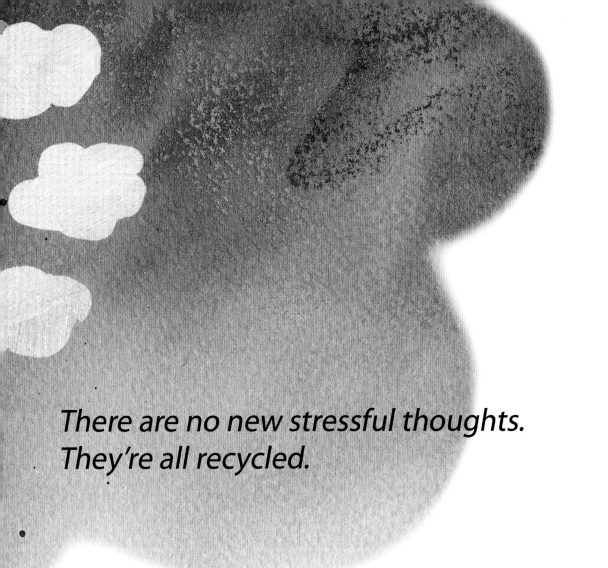

*There are no new stressful thoughts.
They're all recycled.*

If I think you're my problem,

I'm insane.

Who thinks that death is sad? Who thinks that a child shouldn't die? Who thinks that they know what death is? Who tries to teach God, in story after story, thought after thought? Is it you? I say, let's investigate, if you're up for it, and see if it's possible to end the war with reality.

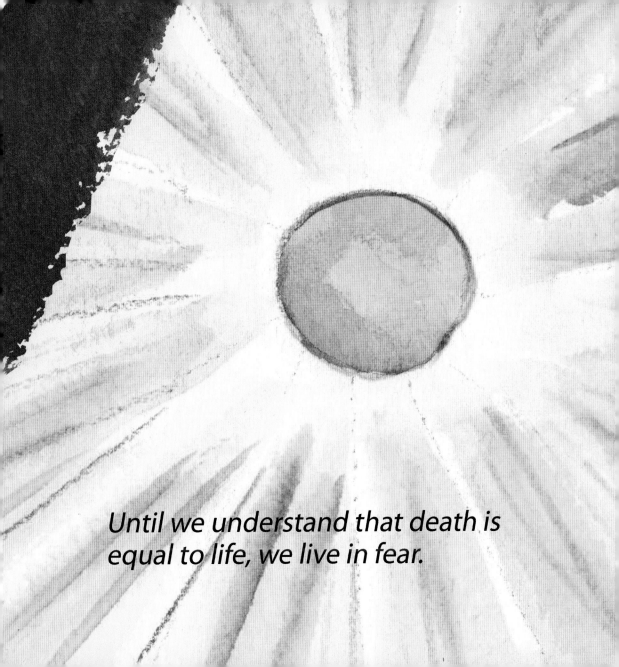

Until we understand that death is equal to life, we live in fear.

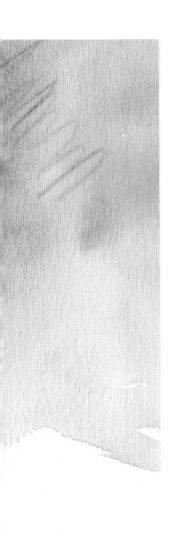

When you question your stressful thoughts, you come to see that everything that has been troubling you is just a misunderstanding.

If you think it was your parents who were out there, you're deluded. There was only God out there, disguised as your parents, giving you what you need. Every time you think your parents should be here for you, don't you experience pain? You miss the reality of it: they're not here! Anytime you think you know what's best for you, it hurts. When you think they should be here when they're over there, you hurt, because the reality of it is that they should be where they are. You're trying to arrange the chessboard, and it has already been done! Checkmate!

Arguing with reality is like trying to teach a cat to bark—hopeless.

*Don't pretend yourself
beyond your evolution.*

"Do I love you?" is the important question. It's the only thing I need to care about. "Do you love me?" is a prison. It's a torture chamber.

*We fear only
what we haven't understood.*

The fear of death is the last smoke screen for the fear of love. The mind looks at nothing and calls it something, to keep from experiencing what it really is. Every fear is the fear of love, because to discover the truth of anything is to discover that there is nobody, no doer, no me, to create suffering or to identify with anything. Without any of that, there is just love.

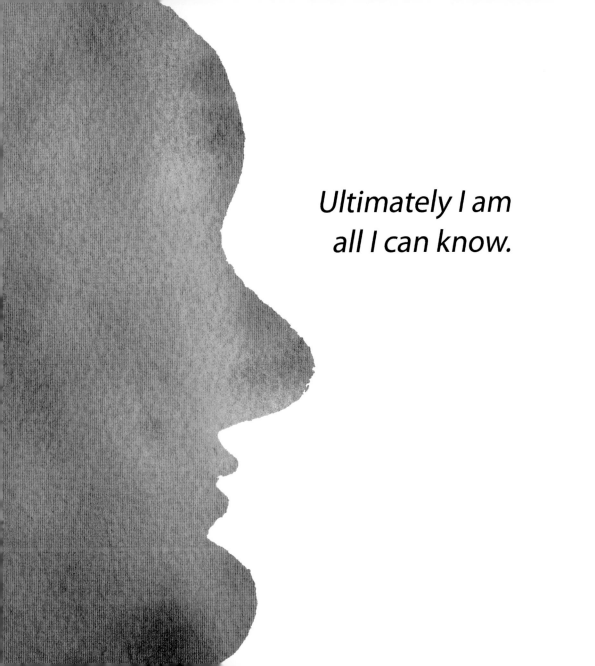

*Ultimately I am
all I can know.*

The litmus test for self-realization is the constant state of gratitude. This gratitude is not something a person can look for or find. It comes from another direction. It takes us over completely. It's so vast that it can't be dimmed or overlaid. It's like its own self. The short version would be: God intoxicated with God, Itself. The total acceptance and consumption of Itself reflected back in the same moment in that central place that is like fusion. It's the beginning. What looks like the end is the beginning. And when you think life is so good that it can't get any better, it gets better. It has to. That's a law.

Gratitude is what we are without a story.

Seeking love keeps you from the awareness that you already have it—that you *are* it.

The ultimate love
is the mind's love of itself.

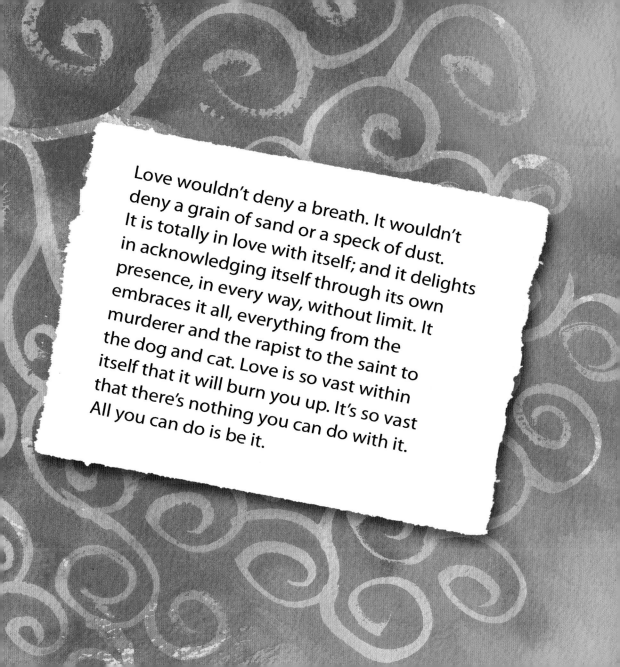

Love wouldn't deny a breath. It wouldn't deny a grain of sand or a speck of dust. It is totally in love with itself; and it delights in acknowledging itself through its own presence, in every way, without limit. It embraces it all, everything from the murderer and the rapist to the saint to the dog and cat. Love is so vast within itself that it will burn you up. It's so vast that there's nothing you can do with it. All you can do is be it.

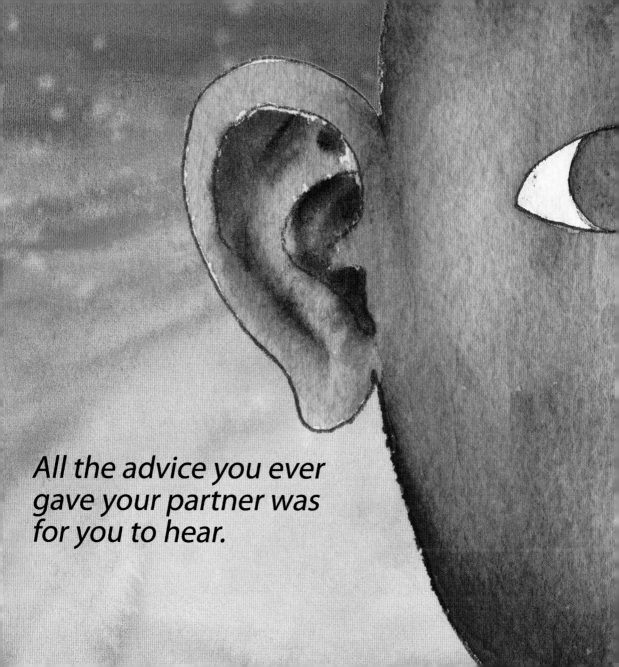

All the advice you ever gave your partner was for you to hear.

Nothing you believe is true.
Knowing this is freedom.

All love songs make sense if we remember what it is that we truly love. If the "you" of a song is another person, then the song is a lie. It has to be, because we can never find our completion in another person. It always comes back to us. So when we put God in the "you" of these songs, we see how true they all are. Every love song is written for God by God.

If you want to see the love of your life, look in the mirror.

How do I know
that I don't need
what I want?
I don't have it.

The Work is about internal cause and effect. It's not about an external world.

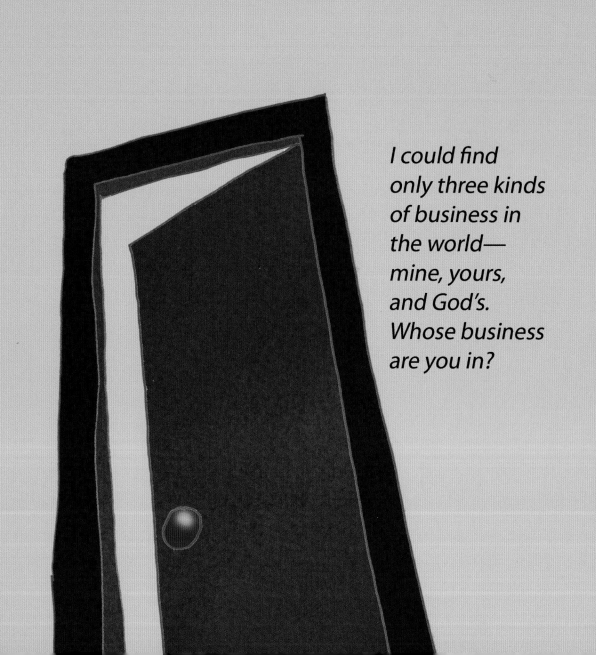

*I could find
only three kinds
of business in
the world—
mine, yours,
and God's.
Whose business
are you in?*

We think that because Jesus and the Buddha wore robes and owned nothing, that's how freedom is supposed to look. But can you live a normal life and be free? Can you do it from here, right now? That's what I want for you. We have the same desire: your freedom. And I love that you're attached to material objects, whether you have them or not, so that you can come to realize that all suffering originates from the mind, not the world.

You are the cause of all the suffering that exists in this world.

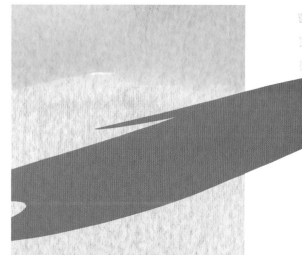

*The key to freedom:
End every judgment
with a question mark.*

The worst loss you've ever experienced is the greatest gift you can have.

We are really alive
only when we live
in nonbelief—
open, waiting,
trusting, and loving
to do what appears
in front of us now.

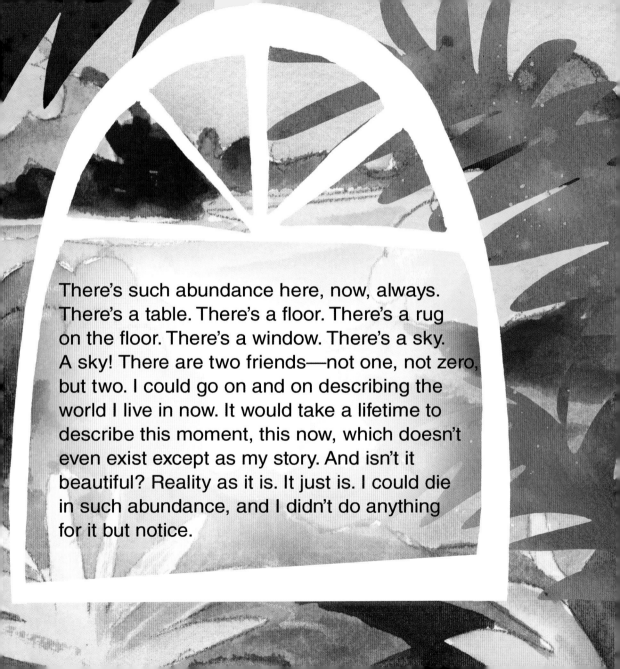

There's such abundance here, now, always.
There's a table. There's a floor. There's a rug
on the floor. There's a window. There's a sky.
A sky! There are two friends—not one, not zero,
but two. I could go on and on describing the
world I live in now. It would take a lifetime to
describe this moment, this now, which doesn't
even exist except as my story. And isn't it
beautiful? Reality as it is. It just is. I could die
in such abundance, and I didn't do anything
for it but notice.

The ego is terrified of the truth.

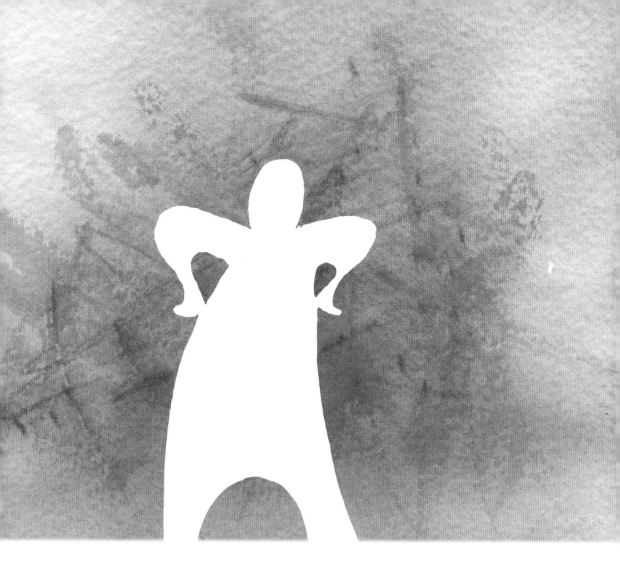

And the truth is that the ego doesn't exist.

Marry yourself and you have married us.
We are you. That's the cosmic joke.

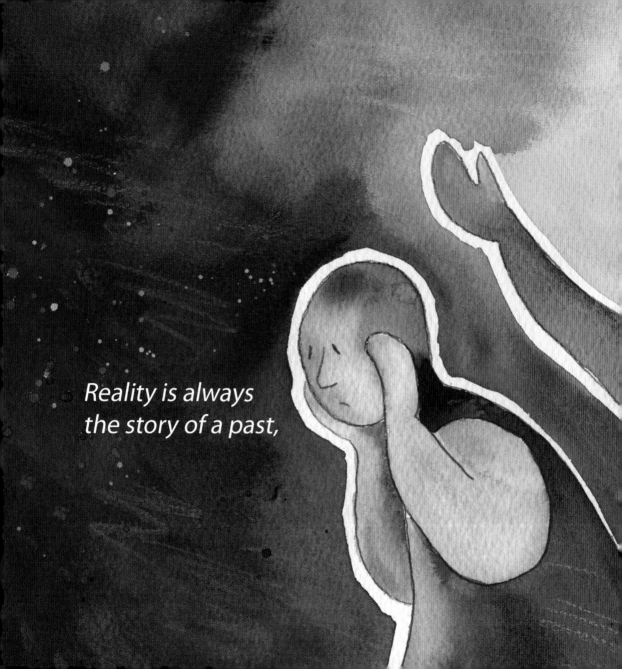

*Reality is always
the story of a past,*

and what I love about
the past is that it's over.

Defense is the first act of war.

I'm very clear that everyone in the world loves me. I just don't expect them to realize it yet.

A thought is harmless until we believe it. It's not our thoughts but our *attachment* to our thoughts that causes suffering.

How would you function if you didn't have your pain and unhappiness? I'm asking you to seriously go inside. How would it be if you smiled all the time, if you were free all the time? It would mean that you wouldn't have control and couldn't manipulate people—that insane idea wouldn't even occur to you. This is how you manipulate: "You should be with me," "If you leave, I'll be miserable." You use these thoughts to get us to agree with your story that there is misery in this world, though the truth is that in your essence you are love, whether you like it or not. You can know that because if you're one thought away from love, you hurt.

Love doesn't seek anything.
It doesn't want, doesn't need,
has no shoulds (not even for
the person's own good).
It's already complete.

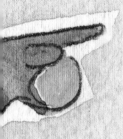

No one has ever been angry at another human being—we're only angry at our *story* about them.

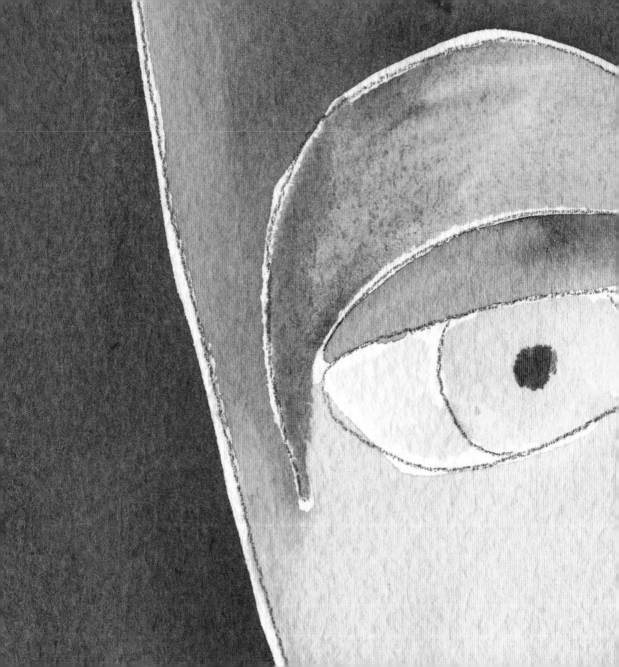

*You can only see what you believe—
nothing else is possible.*

The world is your perception of it.
Inside and outside always match—
they're reflections of each other.
The world is the mirror image of your own mind.

Everyone is a mirror of yourself—
your own thinking coming back at you.

When I am perfectly clear,
what is is what I want.

When we love what is, it becomes so simple to live in the world. The world is exactly as it should be. Everything is God. Everything is good. We're always going to get what we need, not what we think we need. Then we come to see that what we need is not only what we have, it's what we want. Then we come to want only what is. That way, we always win, no matter what.

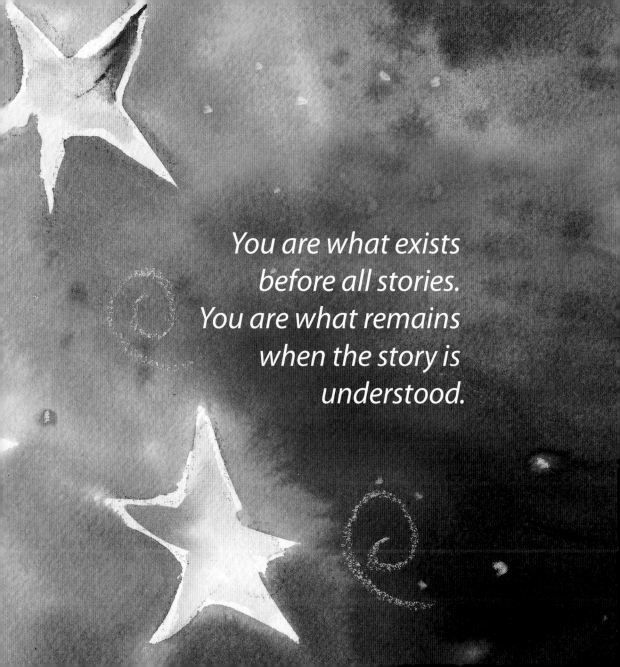

*You are what exists
before all stories.
You are what remains
when the story is
understood.*

My experience is that I'm free. It's how I live internally. I have investigated my thinking, and I discovered that it doesn't mean a thing. I shine with the joy of understanding. I know about suffering, and I know about joy, and I know who I am. I am goodness. That's who we all are. There's no harm here. I would extinguish myself before I would step on an ant intentionally, because I know how to live. With no story, there's nothing to worry about. When there's nothing to do, nowhere to go, no one to be, no past or future, everything feels right. It's all good.

The last story:
God is everything,
God is good.

Byron Katie experienced what she calls "waking up to reality" in 1986, and since then she has introduced The Work, her method of self-inquiry, to millions of people at public events and in prisons, hospitals, churches, VA centers, corporations, universities, and schools. Participants at her nine-day School for The Work and twenty-eight-day residential Turnaround House report profound experiences and lasting transformations. "Katie's events are riveting to watch," the *Times of London* reported. Eckhart Tolle calls The Work "a great blessing for our planet." And *Time* magazine named Katie a "spiritual innovator for the new millennium." Her three bestselling books are *Loving What Is, I Need Your Love — Is That True?*, and *A Thousand Names for Joy.* Visit her online at www.thework.com.

Hans Wilhelm is an award-winning artist and author of over 200 books with total sales of 42 million copies in 30 languages. Visit his website at www.hanswilhelm.com.